FRANCHISING IN ZIMBABWE 2014

Legal and Business Considerations

KENDAL H. TYRE, JR., EXECUTIVE EDITOR
DIANA VILMENAY-HAMMOND, MANAGING EDITOR
COURTNEY L. LINDSAY, II, ASSISTANT EDITOR

LEXNOIR FOUNDATION

FIRST QUARTER 2014

LexNoir Foundation is the charitable, educational arm of LexNoir, an international network of lawyers connecting the African Diaspora.

This publication, *Franchising in Zimbabwe 2014: Legal and Business Considerations*, contains excerpts from *Franchising in Africa 2014: Legal and Business Considerations*. Both works are published by LexNoir Foundation and reflect the points of view of the authors and editors as of the date of publication and do not necessarily represent the opinions, interpretations, or positions of the law firms or organizations with which they are affiliated, nor the opinions, interpretations or positions of LexNoir Foundation or LexNoir.

Nothing contained in this book is to be considered as the rendering of legal advice, either generally or in connection with any specific issues or case. Readers are responsible for obtaining advice from their own legal counsel or other professional. This book, any forms and agreements or other information herein are intended for educational and informational purposes only.

www.lexnoir.org

Table of Contents

Franchising in Zimbabwe

Nellie R.F. Tiyago-Jinjika
Scanlen & Holderness

Bibliography of International Franchise Resources

Kendal H. Tyre, Jr., Diana Vilmenay-Hammond, Pierce Haesung Han, Courtney L. Lindsay II and Keri McWilliams
Nixon Peabody LLP

Acknowledgment

This book could not have been written without the hard work and dedication of each of the contributing authors and editors. Thank you.

We would like to acknowledge and extend our heartfelt gratitude to Michael Collier and Maria Stallings of the Washington, D.C. office of Nixon Peabody LLP for their invaluable assistance in revising, proofing, and editing this publication.

About the Editors and Authors

Kendal H. Tyre, Jr. – Kendal is a partner in the Washington, D.C. office of Nixon Peabody LLP. He handles domestic and cross-border transactions, including mergers and acquisitions, joint ventures, strategic alliances, licensing, and franchise matters.

In his franchise and licensing practice, Kendal counsels domestic and international franchisors, franchisees, licensors, licensees and distributors regarding U.S. state and federal franchise laws as well as foreign franchise legislation in a variety of jurisdictions. Kendal drafts and provides advice with regard to franchise and license agreements, disclosure documents and area development agreements and has extensive experience drafting and negotiating a variety of other commercial agreements. His client base spans the United States and foreign countries, including South Africa, Kenya, and the United Kingdom.

Kendal is a frequent contributor to franchise publications and a frequent speaker at franchise programs held by the American Bar Association Forum on Franchising and the International Franchise Association.

Kendal is co-chair of the firm's Diversity Action Committee and its Africa Group. Kendal is also the executive director of LexNoir Foundation.

E-mail address: ktyre@nixonpeabody.com

Diana Vilmenay-Hammond – Diana is an attorney in the Washington, D.C. office of Nixon Peabody LLP. She is a member of the firm's Franchise & Distribution Team.

In her franchise practice, Diana works with domestic and international franchisors on transactional and litigation matters. Specifically, she counsels franchisor clients regarding state and federal franchise laws, disclosure and registration obligations.

Diana drafts and negotiates various commercial agreements, including international franchise and development agreements.

Diana has co-authored numerous articles on franchising and frequently co-hosted the Nixon Peabody franchise law webinar series. Topics have included:

- "Franchise Case Law Round-Up: Implications for Your Franchise," February 15, 2012;
- "Social Media Part II: Best Practices in Protecting Your Brand in the New Media," September 14, 2010; and
- "The Awuah Case: Bellwether or Outlier," May 11, 2010

Diana received her J.D. from Howard University School of Law and her B.A. from Georgetown University. She is a member of the American Bar Association (Forum on Franchising).

Email address: dvilmenay@nixonpeabody.com

Pierce Haesung Han – Pierce is an associate in Nixon Peabody's Global Business & Transactions Group. Pierce focuses his practice on three main areas, assisting clients with a variety of complex business transactions.

- Mergers & Acquisitions: Providing assistance to both public and private clients with various mergers and acquisitions, performing due diligence, drafting and negotiating transaction documents, and facilitating closing and post-closing mechanics.
- International Commercial Transactions: Drafting and negotiating a variety of commercial agreements, including international franchise and development agreements, license agreements, and purchase and sale agreements.
- Federal Securities Law Matters: Assisting public and private clients regarding federal securities laws and stock exchange rules relating to corporate governance and disclosure.

Pierce serves as the Secretary of the Asian Pacific Bar Association Educational Fund (an affiliate of the Asian Pacific American Bar Association of the Greater Washington, D.C. Area).

Pierce received his J.D. from Georgetown University Law Center and his B.A. from Case Western Reserve University. He is admitted to practice in the State of New York and the District of Columbia.

E-mail address: phan@nixonpeabody.com

Courtney L. Lindsay II – Courtney is an associate in Nixon Peabody's Corporate and Finance practice. In his corporate practice, Courtney assists for-profit and non-profit entities with transactional matters and corporate governance. In various capacities, Courtney has been involved in multiple merger and acquisition transactions, including drafting and managing due diligence.

Previously, Courtney worked in the legal and business affairs department at a national cable network, where he handled matters related to the network's LLC agreement, including drafting board and member consent agreements.

Courtney received his J.D. from the University of Virginia School of Law and his B.A. from the University of Virginia. He is admitted to practice in the Commonwealth of Virginia and the District of Columbia.

E-mail address: clindsay@nixonpeabody.com

Keri McWilliams – Keri is an associate in the Franchise & Distribution team of Nixon Peabody LLP. Keri works with clients on a number of franchising issues, including obtaining and maintaining franchise registrations in various states, responding to state inquiries regarding trade practices, ongoing compliance with state and federal regulations, and updating franchise disclosure documents. She also handles franchise sales counseling and franchise system issues.

Keri is a member of the American Bar Association's Forum on Franchising, and the Federal and Minnesota State bar associations. She is also a member of Minnesota Women Lawyers and the Minnesota Association of Black Lawyers, and a volunteer in the Volunteer Lawyers Network.

Keri received her J.D. from the Georgetown University Law Center and her B.F.A. from Washington University. She is admitted to practice in the District of Columbia and Minnesota.

E-mail address: kmcwilliams@nixonpeabody.com

Nellie R.F. Tiyago-Jinjika – Nellie is a partner at Scanlen & Holderness. Over the years, she has specialized in corporate and commercial law. She has experience in joint ventures, acquisitions, due diligences, drafting and negotiating commercial contracts, commercial litigation and registration of intellectual property. In recent years, Nellie has assisted young Zimbabweans in the establishment of businesses and has advised and provided assistance to foreign and local prospective and actual investors in Zimbabwe.

Nellie is registered as a conveyancer, an administrator registered with the Estate Administration Council of Zimbabwe and is also a member of IBA (International Bar Association). In 2011, the Zimbabwe Institute of Patents and Trademarks Attorneys (ZIPTA) was resuscitated. Nellie served as the Administrator in 2012 and remains a member to date. In addition to being a member of ZIPTA, she is also a member of INTA (International Trademarks Association).

E-mail address: tiyagon@scanlen.co.zw

About the Book

Franchising in Zimbabwe 2014: Legal and Business Considerations contains excerpts from the larger work, *Franchising in Africa 2014: Legal and Business Considerations*. Both books serve as practical, succinct, easy-to-use reference tools for lawyers, business people and academics to use in navigating the myriad laws and business issues impacting franchise arrangements on the African continent.

This book provides an overview of the franchise industry in Zimbabwe and addresses the typical legal issues confronted when expanding a franchise system in Zimbabwe. The larger work, *Franchising in Africa 2014: Legal and Business Considerations*, covers those laws governing franchising in fifteen other African countries – Angola, Botswana, Burundi, Cape Verde, Democratic Republic of Congo, Egypt, Ethiopia, Ghana, Kenya, Mozambique, Nigeria, Rwanda, South Africa, Tunisia and Zambia.

In both books, an author, who is a legal expert in the designated jurisdiction, addresses the basic questions that a franchise lawyer would need to know to competently represent a client in expanding their franchise system to that country.

Each country chapter organizes a discussion of that country's laws under various headings and in a uniform format. Topics were sent to each country's author in the form of a questionnaire, and each author drafted responses to the questions presented. A general overview relating to the political and economic history of the country at the beginning of each chapter provides an initial context for the regulatory framework. [1]

---

[1] The source of information for these sections is the Central Intelligence Agency, https://www.cia.gov/library/publications/the-world-factbook/ (last visited November 3, 2013).

Apart from an overview of the legal framework for franchising, each book contains other articles and resources that should prove useful to those in the franchise industry.

The authors for each chapter are listed at the beginning of a chapter and their biographical information is listed in the previous section, *About the Editors and Authors*.

Readers should always consult with local counsel in the relevant jurisdiction instead of relying solely on the information contained in this book. The laws governing franchising are evolving and local counsel in Zimbabwe are best positioned to provide timely, relevant advice applying the current law to the particular facts of a case.

Franchising in Zimbabwe

Nellie R.F. Tiyago-Jinjika

Scanlen & Holderness

Harare, Zimbabwe

Zimbabwe

I.   Introduction

A.   Historical Background of Country

In 1965, Zimbabwe ceased to be a British colony after the Unilateral Declaration of Independence. Zimbabwe, then known as Rhodesia, remained under the rule of the minority white population. A civil war ensued between the British colonialists and black national freedom fighters in 1965 and eventually ended with the signing of the Lancaster House Agreement in 1979. The agreement facilitated the holding of elections and, on April 18, 1980, Robert Mugabe became the first elected Prime Minister of the new Zimbabwe. General elections held in March 2008 amounted to a censure of the Zimbabwe African National Union – Patriotic Front-led government with the opposition winning a majority of seats in parliament. The Movement for Democratic Change Zimbabwe opposition leader Morgan Tsvangirai won the most votes in the presidential polls, but not enough to win outright. Difficult negotiations over a power-sharing government, in which Mugabe remained president and Tsvangirai became prime minister, were finally settled in February 2009, although the leaders failed to agree upon many key outstanding governmental issues. Since then there have been numerous elections held with the final elections resulting in the ruling party, Zimbabwe African National Union – Patriotic Front (ZANU PF) remaining in power after what has been globally called the "free and fair" elections of Zimbabwe.

B.   Economy of the Country

Zimbabwe's economy is growing despite continuing political uncertainty. Following a decade of contraction from 1998 to 2008, Zimbabwe's economy recorded real growth of more than 9% per year in 2010-11, before slowing to 5% in 2012, due in part to a poor harvest and low diamond revenues. The government of Zimbabwe still faces a number of difficult economic problems, including infrastructure and regulatory deficiencies, policy uncertainty, a large external debt burden, and insufficient formal employment. Due to extreme hyperinflation a

1

Zimbabwe

multi-currency economy was introduced in February 2009 – which allowed currencies such as the Botswana pula, the South Africa rand, and the US dollar to be used locally. This ended hyperinflation and reduced inflation to about 10%.

C.   Franchise Legal Overview

Franchise agreements are governed by the laws of Zimbabwe with no specific law that strictly regulates franchising itself. The laws that are applicable to all businesses in Zimbabwe are applied to the business of franchising. Of note are the company laws, indigenization laws, investment laws, competition laws and tax laws.

In Zimbabwe, indigenization laws prescribe that any business conducted in Zimbabwe that meets certain thresholds should be controlled by indigenous people. The laws also prescribe industries which have been reserved to indigenous Zimbabweans and cannot be ventured into without approval.[2]

---

[2] On March 9, 2008, Zimbabwe's President, Robert Mugabe signed the Indigenization and Economic Empowerment Bill into law. The law requires that controlling interest in businesses and business ventures in Zimbabwe revert to indigenous Zimbabweans that were previously disadvantaged before 1980. The act provides for manners in which indigenization may be achieved including points for socio economic projects and community and employee share trust. It further allows the Minister of Indigenization to exercise his discretion when presented with an indigenization plan where there will be a substantial benefit to the Zimbabwean economy. Thresholds have been set for various industries but the general rule is that if a business has a net value of US$500,000 or less, there is no need to indigenize. The threshold for a business in the mining sector is US$1. There are specific sectors of industry that have been reserved for indigenous persons and to enter into these one has to seek the necessary approval from the Zimbabwe Investment Authority and Minister of Indigenization. At the moment the following sectors are reserved: agriculture (primary production of food and cash crops); transportation (passenger buses, taxes and car and car hire services); retail and wholesale trade; barber shops, hairdressing and beauty salons; employment agencies; estate agencies; valet services; grain milling; bakeries; tobacco grading and packaging; tobacco processing; advertising agencies; milk processing and provision of local arts craft, marketing and distribution.

Zimbabwe

II. Regulatory Requirements

A. Pre-Sale Disclosure

Please describe any pre-sale franchise disclosure or similar requirements that may apply to franchise transactions.

No pre-sale franchise disclosure or similar requirements apply to franchise transactions under the laws of Zimbabwe.

B. Governmental Approvals, Registrations, Filing Requirements

Please describe any necessary government approvals, registrations, or filing requirements that may apply to franchise transactions.

Generally where one is to enter into an agreement that will place an obligation on it to make payments outside Zimbabwe, exchange control regulations as explained in III (Currency) below, must be complied with. Filing requirements as discussed in detail in V (Trademarks) below must also be complied with.

Even though government approval is not specifically required for entering into a franchise agreement, local courts have held that the government has the power to intervene and influence the ambit of a franchise agreement. This has been done before where the Government of Zimbabwe intervened to nationalize the motor industry.[3]

C. Limits of Fees and Typical Term of Franchise Agreement

Please describe any limits upon the nature and extent of fees and the term of a typical franchise agreement.

---

[3]   *Acting Minister of Industry and Technology and Another v Tanaka Power (Private) Limited 1990* (2) ZLR 208 Supreme Court.

Zimbabwe

As there is no specific law governing franchising, parties are free to agree on the terms and conditions of a franchise agreement subject to the laws in Zimbabwe that govern relationships between parties as detailed above.

III. Currency

If all payments under a franchise agreement must be made in immediately available U.S. Dollars, please advise as to any restrictions, reporting requirements, or regulations concerning the exchange, repatriation, or remittance of U.S. Dollars.

Bank regulations require that payments in foreign currency with funds to be remitted outside Zimbabwe must first obtain prior approval of the Reserve Bank of Zimbabwe. In the event that a party binds itself without obtaining prior approval out of ignorance of the law, the approval may be applied for after the fact. Approval is obtained by application made through authorized dealers, which are usually the registered banks who will advise of the requirements at the time of application.

The banking laws also recognize directives from the Governor of the Reserve Bank of Zimbabwe as legally binding on persons conducting business in Zimbabwe. Therefore, one must ensure that there is compliance with the directives as they are published from time to time.

Zimbabwe also subscribes to international anti-money laundering requirements and as such all transactions involving receipt and remittance of money must be conducted through the normal banking channels. Should a bank be suspicious of the activity in an account, they have the power to freeze such account without prior notice to the account holder.

IV. Taxes, Tariffs, and Duties

Please do not provide any in-depth comments on tax structuring. However, please provide your general comments on the typical amount of withholding tax that would apply and whether a

Zimbabwe

"gross-up" provision contained in a franchise agreement would be enforceable in your country.

Below is an overview of the tax applicable to the non-resident Franchisor.

A.   Applicable Rate

Dividends may be subject to non-resident sales tax depending on the terms of any double taxation agreements with the country of residence of the recipient.

A non-resident recipient of interest from a source in Zimbabwe may be liable to income tax in Zimbabwe on such interest. Taxable interest also includes interest payable by a person who is ordinarily resident or carries on business in Zimbabwe.

In addition, non-residents may be liable to withholding tax on fees, royalties and remittances to a country outside Zimbabwe. The current applicable withholding tax rate is 10%.

Presently, Zimbabwe has double taxation agreements with the United Kingdom, Germany, Netherlands and South Africa.

B.   Gross-up Clauses

Gross-up provisions are practiced and permitted under the laws of Zimbabwe.

V.   Trademarks

Please advise us as to whether there are any special requirements for granting a valid trademark license, including the use of a registered user agreement or a short trademark license agreement and any required filing of such an agreement with the trademark authorities.

The registration of marks is governed by the Trade Marks Act 26:04, which prescribes the manner in which marks are to be

Zimbabwe

registered in Zimbabwe. This includes filing of an application with copies of the mark to be registered and payment of the prescribed fee. The mark to be registered is published in the Trademarks Journal, after which it is sealed and registered if no objection to the registration is raised. A mark successfully registered will be protected for a renewable 10 year period.

The proprietor of a registered mark may apply to the Registrar of Trade Marks for registration of another person as a registered user under terms of the Trade Marks Act. A registered use application must be submitted to the Registrar by both the user and the owner, and must state the particulars of the relationship, the goods covered, and the conditions of the use. The following items are required to record a license:

(1) a registered user or license agreement;

(2) forms of authorization from the owner and user (equal to a power of attorney); and

(3) a declaration and statement of case from the owner or the registered user describing the circumstances, terms and conditions of use associated with the license.[4]

Finally, Zimbabwe is the headquarters for ARIPO (African Regional Intellectual Property Organisation). ARIPO has eighteen member states in Africa.[5] Application for registration of one's mark or patent will result in protection in the states chosen by the applicant.

---

[4]   See also Edward Fennessy and International Contributors, *Trademarks Throughout the World, Fifth Edition, Release #18* 181-17, THOMAS REUTERS/WEST, (2012).

[5]   The following countries are currently members of ARIPO: Botswana, the Gambia, Ghana, Kenya, Lesotho, Malawi, Mozambique, Namibia, Sierra Leone, Liberia, Rwanda, Somalia, Sudan, Swaziland, Tanzania, Uganda, Zambia and Zimbabwe

Zimbabwe

VI. Restrictions on Transfer

Please advise as to whether there are any restrictions (1) on a franchisor to restrict transfers by a master franchisee, any interest in a master franchisee, or the assets of the master franchisee or (2) the ability of a master franchisee to control and/or restrict transfers of a subfranchisee's rights under a master franchise agreement, interest in the subfranchisee, or the assets of the subfranchisee.

In relation to a Master Franchise and Subfranchise:

A. Assignment

Parties may agree on assignment provisions provided that they comply with the laws of Zimbabwe and are not deemed to be contrary to public policy.

B. Change of Control

Change of control of any Zimbabwean registered entity requires compliance with the indigenization laws and competition laws.

C. Transfer of Assets

Parties may agree on the timing and manner in which assets will be transferred. The valuation formula may be predetermined by the parties. Any funds transferred in connection with asset transfers must be processed through the proper banking channels. Of note are laws in Zimbabwe that prohibit non-Zimbabweans from participating in hire purchase arrangements.[6]

---

[6] Hire purchase agreements are those that allow a party to purchase property through installments. Ownership of the property does not transfer until all payments are satisfied.

VII. Termination

Please advise us as to any laws relating to termination in your country, such as agency laws, required indemnity provisions, notice or "good cause" requirements, or other laws affecting termination of a franchise agreement. Please describe.

Termination is dependent on the agreement between parties. Where termination is by virtue of breach of contract, it is common to have a notice period provided for in the agreement. Alternatively, an agreement can be worded in such a manner as to automatically terminate upon occurrence or non-occurrence of certain events. Consequences of termination must be in compliance with the laws.

VIII. Governing Law, Jurisdiction, and Dispute Resolution

A.   Choice of Law of Foreign Jurisdiction

Please confirm whether the choice of law of a foreign jurisdiction would likely to be upheld under the law of the country, except for certain matters such as trademarks, bankruptcy, and competition matters, which we assume would be governed by the law in your country.

Parties may choose a particular jurisdiction to govern their agreement, including a foreign jurisdiction. The parties must consider which jurisdiction will provide them with effective and timely resolution of any disputes.

B.   International Arbitration Dispute Resolution

Please confirm that a court in your country would honor an election of international arbitration dispute resolution, and therefore refuse to hear any disputes arising under a franchise agreement.

Zimbabwe

Arbitrations in Zimbabwe are governed by the Arbitration Act Chapter 7:15, which was enacted to give effect to domestic and international arbitration agreements. In addition, the Arbitration Act applies, with modifications, the Model Law on International Commercial Arbitration as adopted by the United Nations Commission on International Trade Law on June, 21, 1985.

It is important that parties should have an exhaustive arbitration clause that will detail selection of arbitrators and procedures to be followed during the arbitration to avoid an abuse of the arbitration process. In addition, it must be specifically agreed that the decision of the arbitrator is final and binding on the parties.

Zimbabwe is not a signatory to the *Convention on the Recognition and Enforcement of Foreign Arbitral Awards* (the "New York Convention").

IX.   Non-Competition Provisions

If the franchise agreement prohibits the master franchisee from engaging in certain competitive activities during the term of the agreement, and for a 12-month period after the termination or expiration of the agreement, please comment on the enforceability of non-competition covenants in your country.

Provisions that prohibit or restrict competition are not allowed under the competition laws of Zimbabwe. The Competition Act Chapter 14:28 aims to promote and maintain competition in the economy of Zimbabwe, to provide for the prevention and control of restrictive practices, to prevent and control of monopoly situations and prohibit unfair trade practices.

A non-compete clause will generally be regarded as a penalty clause which one can challenge both in terms of contract law and competition laws.

X.   Language Requirements

Does the law in your country require that a franchise agreement be translated into the local language in order to be enforceable between the parties?

Zimbabwe is an English speaking country with a very high literacy rate. Agreements are valid regardless of the language they may be entered into. It is prudent to have a certified translation of agreements which may from time to time be required by relevant authorities.

XI.   Other Significant Matters

Please advise as to whether there are any significant matters not addressed above of which a franchisor should be aware in connection with its entering into a franchise agreement in your country.

There are no other significant matters to be discussed.

Bibliography of International Franchise Resources

Kendal H. Tyre, Jr., Diana Vilmenay-Hammond, Pierce Haesung Han, Courtney L. Lindsay II and Keri McWilliams

Nixon Peabody LLP

Washington, D.C.

I. General International Resources

Mark Abell, Gary R. Duvall, and Andrea Oricchio Kirsh, *International Franchise Legislation* B1, ABA FORUM ON FRANCHISING (1996)

Kathleen C. Anderson and Anthony M. Stiegler, *Put Muscle in Your Marks: Enforcing Intellectual Property Rights* W14, ABA FORUM ON FRANCHISING (1995)

Richard M. Asbill and Jane W. LaFranchi, *International Franchise Sales Laws—A Survey* W7, ABA FORUM ON FRANCHISING (2005)

Jeffery A. Brimer, Alison C. McElroy, and John Pratt, *Going International: What Additional Restraints Will You Face?* W4, ABA FORUM ON FRANCHISING (2011)

Michael G. Brennan, Alexander Konigsberg, and Philip F. Zeidman, *Globetrotting: A Workshop on International Franchising* 10/W8, ABA FORUM ON FRANCHISING (1994)

Michael G. Brennan, Alexander Konigsberg, and Philip F. Zeidman, *Globetrotting: Strategies for Launching U.S. Franchisors Abroad* 2/P2, ABA FORUM ON FRANCHISING (1994)

Christopher P. Bussert and Jennifer Dolman, *Regaining Your Trademark After Abandonment or Misappropriation* W7, ABA FORUM ON FRANCHISING (2011)

Ronald T. Coleman and Linda K. Stevens, *Trade Secrets and Confidential Information: Rights and Remedies* W2, ABA FORUM ON FRANCHISING (2000)

Finola Cunningham, *Commerce Department Helps Franchisors Go Global*, in FRANCHISING WORLD 63 (Dec. 2005)

Michael R. Daigle and Alex S. Konigsberg, *Meeting Off-Shore Disclosure and Contract Requirements* F/W13, ABA FORUM ON FRANCHISING (1992)

Jennifer Dolman, Robert A. Lauer, and Lawrence M. Weinberg, *Structuring International Master Franchise Relationships for Success and Responding When Things Go Awry* W22, ABA FORUM ON FRANCHISING (2007)

Gary R. Duvall, Paul Jones, and Jane LaFranchi, *Planning for the International Enforcement of Franchise Agreements* W6, ABA FORUM ON FRANCHISING (1999)

William Edwards, *International Expansion: Do Opportunities Outweigh Challenges?* in FRANCHISING WORLD (February 2008)

George J. Eydt and Stuart Hershman, *Bringing a Foreign Franchise System to the United States* W9, ABA FORUM ON FRANCHISING (2009)

William A. Finkelstein and Louis T. Pirkey, *International Trademarks* W15, ABA FORUM ON FRANCHISING (1991)

William A. Finkelstein, *Protecting Trademarks Internationally: Current Strategies and Developments* B3, ABA FORUM ON FRANCHISING (1996)

Stephen Giles, Lou H. Jones, and Lawrence Weinberg, *Negotiating and Documenting Complex International Franchise Agreements* W21, ABA FORUM ON FRANCHISING (2006)

Steven M. Goldman, Stephen Giles, Marc Israel, and Stanley Wong, *Competition Round Up from Around the World* LB2, ABA FORUM ON FRANCHISING (2004)

David C. Gryce and E. Lynn Perry, *Trademarks and Copyrights in the International Arena* 6/W4, ABA FORUM ON FRANCHISING (1993)

Kenneth S. Kaplan, Andrew P. Loewinger, and Penelope J. Ward, *System Standards in International Franchising* W14, ABA FORUM ON FRANCHISING (2005)

Edward Levitt and Jorge Mondragon, *A Survey of International Legal Traps and How to Avoid Them—Beyond the Franchise Laws* W20, ABA FORUM ON FRANCHISING (2007)

Ned Levitt, Kendal H. Tyre, and Penny Ward, *The Impossible Dream: Controlling Your International Franchise System* W4, ABA FORUM ON FRANCHISING (2010)

Michael K. Lindsey and Andrew P. Loewinger, *International (Non-U.S.) Franchise Disclosure Requirements* W9, ABA FORUM ON FRANCHISING (2002)

Andrew P. Loewinger and John Pratt, *Recent Changes and Trends in International Franchise Laws* W4, ABA FORUM ON FRANCHISING (2008)

Andrew P. Loewinger and Thomas M. Pitegoff, *Avoiding the Long Arm of the Law in International Franchising: Issues and Approaches* W8, ABA FORUM ON FRANCHISING (1995)

Craig J. Madson and Katherine C. Spelman, *Similarity and Confusion in the Intellectual Property Arena* W11, ABA FORUM ON FRANCHISING (1997)

Christopher A. Nowak, John Pratt, and Carl E. Zwisler, *Franchising Internationally with Countries with Opaque Legal Systems* W20, ABA FORUM ON FRANCHISING (2006)

E. Lynn Perry and John L. Sullivan Jr., *Trademark Compliance and Enforcement Techniques* E/W12, ABA FORUM ON FRANCHISING (1992)

Marcel Portmann, *Franchising Sector Proves Global Reach*, in FRANCHISING WORLD (January 2007)

John Pratt and Luiz Henrique O. do Amaral, *Civil Law for Common Law Practitioners (or How to Draft an Agreement for Use Overseas)* W4, ABA FORUM ON FRANCHISING (2002)

Kirk W. Reilly, Robert F. Salkowski and Geoffrey B. Shaw, *Determining the Rules of Engagement in Litigation Here and Abroad* W5, ABA FORUM ON FRANCHISING (2008)

Catherine Riesterer and Frank Zaid, *Basics of International Franchising* L/B2, ABA FORUM ON FRANCHISING (1997)

W. Andrew Scott and Christopher N. Wormald, *Stranger in a Strange Land: Contrasting Franchising in International Expansion* W2, ABA FORUM ON FRANCHISING (2003)

Donald Smith and Erik Wulff, *International Franchising: The Unraveling of an International Franchise Relationship* 15/W13, ABA FORUM ON FRANCHISING (1993)

Frank Zaid, Pamela Mills, and Michael Santa Maria, *Essential Issues in International Franchising* LB/1, ABA FORUM ON FRANCHISING (2001)

II. African Resources

Joyce G. Mazero and J. Perry Maisonneuve, *Franchising in the Middle East and North Africa* W2, ABA FORUM ON FRANCHISING (2009)

Kendal H. Tyre, Jr. and Diana Vilmenay-Hammond, *Franchise World: A Burgeoning Middle Class Spurs Franchise Investment in Africa*, MINORITY BUSINESS ENTREPRENEUR (November 2012)

Kendal H. Tyre, Jr., *IP Protection May Promote Additional Franchise Growth in Africa*, NIXON PEABODY LLP: FRANCHISING BUSINESS & LAW ALERT (September 2012)

Kendal H. Tyre, Jr., *Market Potential for Franchising in Africa*, NIXON PEABODY LLP: FRANCHISING BUSINESS & LAW ALERT (June 2011)

Kendal H. Tyre, Jr. and Courtney L. Lindsay, II, *Continued Growth of Franchising in Africa*, NIXON PEABODY LLP: FRANCHISE LAW ALERT (April 2013)

Kendal H. Tyre, Jr. and Courtney L. Lindsay, II, *Pan African Franchise Federation Holds Inaugural Meeting*, NIXON PEABODY LLP: AFRICA ALERT (June 2013)

Kendal H. Tyre, Jr. and Courtney L. Lindsay, II, *White House Encouraging Private Investment and Transparency in Sub-Saharan Africa*, NIXON PEABODY LLP: AFRICA ALERT (August 2012)

Kendal H. Tyre, Jr. and Diana Vilmenay-Hammond, *African Economic Growth Impacts Franchising on the Continent*, NIXON PEABODY LLP: FRANCHISE LAW ALERT (July 2012)

Kendal H. Tyre, Jr. and Diana Vilmenay-Hammond, *Franchising in Africa*, in FRANCHISING WORLD (August 2013)

John Sotos and Sam Hall, *African Franchising: Cross-Continent Momentum*, in FRANCHISING WORLD (June 2007)

A.   Angola

João Afonso Fialho, *Franchising in Angola*, in FRANCHISING IN AFRICA: LEGAL AND BUSINESS CONSIDERATIONS 91-105 (Kendal H. Tyre, Jr. & Diana Vilmenay-Hammond eds. 2012)

B.   Botswana

Bonzo Makgalemele, *Franchising in Botswana*, in FRANCHISING IN AFRICA: LEGAL AND BUSINESS CONSIDERATIONS 107-117 (Kendal H. Tyre, Jr. & Diana Vilmenay-Hammond eds. 2012)

C.   Cape Verde

João Afonso Fialho, *Franchising in Cape Verde*, in FRANCHISING IN AFRICA: LEGAL AND BUSINESS CONSIDERATIONS 119-132 (Kendal H. Tyre, Jr. & Diana Vilmenay-Hammond eds. 2012)

D.   Egypt

Girgis Abd El-Shahid, *Franchising in Eqypt*, in FRANCHISING IN AFRICA: LEGAL AND BUSINESS CONSIDERATIONS 133-142 (Kendal H. Tyre, Jr. & Diana Vilmenay-Hammond eds. 2012)

A. Safaa El Din El Oteifi, *Egypt*, in INTERNATIONAL FRANCHISING EGY/1 (Dennis Campbell gen. ed. 2011)

E.   Ethiopia

Yohannes Assefa and Biset Beyene Molla, *Franchising in Ethiopia*, in FRANCHISING IN AFRICA: LEGAL AND BUSINESS CONSIDERATIONS 143-157 (Kendal H. Tyre, Jr. & Diana Vilmenay-Hammond eds. 2012)

Kendal H. Tyre, Jr., Yohannes Assefa and Getachew Mengistie Alemu, *New Intellectual Property Regulation Requires Scramble to Protect Marks in Ethiopia*, NIXON PEABODY LLP: AFRICA ALERT (October 2013)

F.   Ghana

Divine K.D. Letsa and Hawa Tejansie Ajei, *Franchising in Ghana*, in FRANCHISING IN AFRICA: LEGAL AND BUSINESS CONSIDERATIONS 159-167 (Kendal H. Tyre, Jr. & Diana Vilmenay-Hammond eds. 2012)

G.   Libya

Kendal H. Tyre, Jr. & Diana Vilmenay-Hammond, *First U.S. Franchise Opens in Libya*, NIXON PEABODY LLP: AFRICA ALERT (August 2012)

H.   Mozambique

Diogo Xavier da Cunha, *Franchising in Mozambique*, in FRANCHISING IN AFRICA: LEGAL AND BUSINESS CONSIDERATIONS 169-182 (Kendal H. Tyre, Jr. & Diana Vilmenay-Hammond eds. 2012)

I.   Nigeria

Theo Emuwa and Bimbola Fowler-Ekar, *Franchising in Nigeria*, in FRANCHISING IN AFRICA: LEGAL AND BUSINESS CONSIDERATIONS 183-198 (Kendal H. Tyre, Jr. & Diana Vilmenay-Hammond eds. 2012)

Kendal H. Tyre, Jr. and Theo Emuwa, *Nigerian Franchising: Making Your Way Through the Thicket*, NIXON PEABODY LLP: FRANCHISE LAW ALERT (June 2005)

J.   South Africa

Eugene Honey, *Franchising and the New Consumer Protection Bill*, BOWMAN GILFILLAN (March 2008)

Eugene Honey, *Franchising and the Consumer Protection Bill*, BOWMAN GILFILLAN (May 2008)

Eugene Honey, *Pitfalls and Difficulties with the CPA*, ADAMS & ADAMS (March 2013)

Eugene Honey, *Disclosure is Compulsory*, ADAMS & ADAMS (May 2013)

Eugene Honey and Wim Alberts, *Fundamental Consumer Rights: The Right to Equality*, BOWMAN GILFILLAN (March 2009)

Eugene Honey and Wim Alberts, *The Reach of the Consumer Protection Bill: The Final*, BOWMAN GILFILLAN (March 2009)

Eugene Honey, *South Africa*, in GETTING THE DEAL THROUGH: FRANCHISE (2013) 172-178 (Philip F. Zeidman ed. 2013)

Taswell Papier, *Franchising in South Africa*, in FRANCHISING IN AFRICA: LEGAL AND BUSINESS CONSIDERATIONS 199-224 (Kendal H. Tyre, Jr. & Diana Vilmenay-Hammond eds. 2012)

Kendal H. Tyre, Jr., *A New Legal Landscape for Franchising in South Africa*, NIXON PEABODY LLP: FRANCHISING BUSINESS & LAW ALERT (September 2009)

K.　Tunisia

Yessine Ferah, *Franchising in Tunisia*, in FRANCHISING IN AFRICA: LEGAL AND BUSINESS CONSIDERATIONS 225-245 (Kendal H. Tyre, Jr. & Diana Vilmenay-Hammond eds. 2012)

Kendal H. Tyre, Jr., Diana Vilmenay-Hammond, and Yessine Ferah, *New Franchise Legislation in Tunisia*, NIXON PEABODY LLP: FRANCHISE LAW ALERT (September 2010)

L.　Zambia

Mabvuto Sakala, *Franchising in Zambia*, in FRANCHISING IN AFRICA: LEGAL AND BUSINESS CONSIDERATIONS 247-255 (Kendal H. Tyre, Jr. & Diana Vilmenay-Hammond eds. 2012)

14736317.2